MISCELLANEOUS THOUGHTS

POETRY

V. M. SANG

OTHER BOOKS BY V.M.SANG

Fiction

The Wolves of Vimar series

The Wolf Pack

The Never-Dying Man

Wolf Moon

The Wolves of Vimar prequels

Jovinda and Noli

The Making of a Mage

Dreams of an Elf Maid

Elemental Worlds Duo

The Stones of Earth and Air

The Stones of Fire and Water

A Family Through the Ages

Vengeance of a Slave

Jealousy of a Viking

Non-Fiction

Viv's Family Recipes

PREFACE

When I was a student in Manchester, England, I wrote some poetry. Most of those poems have now been lost in the intervening years. Only one survives.

Then, many years later, the school where I worked had a staff Christmas dinner and some people agreed to act as entertainment after the meal. We had earlier had a rather disastrous visit to France with a group of fourteen-year-olds. A few things went wrong and so I wrote a humorous poem about the trip. It was met with approval and over the next ten years or so, I wrote other poems, mainly about the doings at the school.

Unfortunately, these have also been lost except for one about the National Lottery, which I've published here. Anyway, since most of those poems were about events no one else knew much about except the staff of the school, I would probably not have published them anyway.

I hope you enjoy my little book. If you do, please leave a comment on Amazon. Reviews are important for authors and readers. They help readers to get an idea as to whether they would like the book or not, and they help the author become better known. It's one of the greatest gifts you can give to your favourite authors.

SEASONS AND FESTIVALS

SPRING

I thought I'd write some poems about the seasons. Here is one about spring.

Dandelions, like gold, cover the meadows.
Newborn lambs frolic in fields.
New leaves on the trees are casting their shadows
And winter's cold grip quickly yields.

At the edges of woodland the primroses glow
And cowslips their scent fills the air.
Anemones dance when the breezes do blow
And birds sing with never a care.

Then bluebells and campions come into bloom
Their colour the blue of the sea.
The cuckoo, that herald of spring, will come soon,
His call echoing over the lea.

The song of the blackbird is like molten gold.
His notes are so pure and so clear.
Hearing him seems to banish the cold
And brings joy to all those who hear.

Robin is nesting, and other birds too,
The hedgehog is active once more.
The young of the deer and the badger and shrew
Play their games as in old days of yore.

The sun climbs higher and higher each day
Giving more of his heat and his light.
It sparkles like stars fallen into the bay.
All smile at the beautiful sight.

Hope and excitement come with each spring morn.
What blessings will come with this day?
New starts can begin once again with each dawn
And send us all hopeful away.

SOUNDS OF SUMMER

For me, summer is about the sounds. The buzzing of bees, the song of the birds, laughter of children playing on the beach.

Blackbird sings from highest bough;
His notes tumble to us below.
Like golden honey, his song is sweet
Giving our ears a wonderful treat.

Skylark rises above the fields
By his waterfall song all sorrows are healed
Higher and higher, he rises until
We no longer can see him, nor hear his trill.

The drone of the bee fills the silence at noon.
In the heat of the day, all are resting at home.
But her buzzing tells us that she will not rest
Searching for flowers is her favourite quest.

Two stones rapped together? What is this sound?
If you look very hard, a stonechat can be found.
His chat-chat song is quiet and soft;
It's easily missed. A shame to be lost.

A splash as a child runs into the sea.
The cry of the gulls soaring high above me.
The call of the curlew up on the moors
As he flies up high over heather and gorse.

The farmers are cutting the hay and the corn,
Rising so early before it is dawn.
The sound of the harvester now fills the air.
It has to be finished before autumn is there.

Summer is sounds and the sun rising high
Beating his rays down out of the sky.
Summer is birdsong and scents of the hay
And sunlight that lasts throughout the long day.

Autumn in Sussex

I moved to Sussex in 2002. I love walking on the Downs, but there are many flat walks too if you don't feel like hills.

The Downs are wreathed in mist, like smoke
From a dying fire.
The leaves are turning red and gold
Like flames upon a pyre.

Spring's little lambs are grown to sheep
The swallows they have flown.
The blossoms that the summer brought
Their petals all have thrown.

Now autumn's bounty fills the woods,
The hedgerows are ablaze
With hips and haws in colours bright
The senses to amaze.

The smoke from wood fires fills the air,
The scent of autumn true.
The autumn sun is cooler now
And mornings filled with dew.

The cobwebs shine with dewdrops bright.
The spider in her lair
Thinks nothing of the rainbow hue
That scatters in the air.

And children kick the fallen leaves
As laughingly they run
To gather conkers, shiny brown,
Gleaming in the sun.

We gather blackberries from the hedge
And apples from on high.
Up in the tree they ripen now
To turn into a pie.

But autumn sometimes has a kick
And the rain it lashes down.
The wind, it howls within the eaves
And through the trees doth moan.

WINTER NIGHT

These two poems were written as more of my seasonal poems.

Snow covers the ice-hard ground
And ponds and lakes are frozen.
All is muffled, every sound.
The birds are silent in the trees,
No moths or butterflies or bees
Just snowflakes by the dozen.

The moon is full and her pale light
Shines gently through the flakes.
But creatures shiver through the night.
The icy wind makes branches quiver
And every living thing to shiver
In trees and hills and lakes.

Across the field there trots a fox.
An owl flies by on silent wings.
On the frozen lake, some ducks.
As snow falls gently on them all,
And cattle low within their stall
We are waiting for the spring.

WINTER

Everything dead.
Nothing moves.
The skies of lead
Press down on the roofs.

The icicles hang
Like teeth in the maw.
Each one a fang
In a wolf's jaw.

The wind with his knife
Cuts through to the bone.
Soon snow will arrive
And the swallows have flown.

The trees that were green
Are now turned to white,
And everything's seen
In a glowing bright light.

But look what I've found!
A tiny green shoot
Pushing up through the ground.
A snowdrop, no doubt.

It tells of the spring
Not so far away,
And how it will bring
All the flowers of May.

THE STORM

I was staying in Germany, near Leipzig in order to go to a concert in the Thomaskirke. On our way back to the hotel, there was a tremendous thunderstorm. I was inspired to write the following poem.

A lovely day, the sun was warm
It had shone on us since dawn.
The heat oppressed us all the day,
Even as in bed we lay.

We went to Leipzig in the heat.
In Thomaskirke we took our seat
To hear St John by J.S.Bach.
It did not end till after dark.

When we emerged it was in rain.
We rushed to find our car again.
The thunder rolled across the sky,
The lightning flashed, but now we're dry.

We drove toward Chemnitz and saw
O'er Dresden, flashes like the War.
Was it '45 again
With the bombs falling like the rain?

The lightning flashed, the thunder boomed.
We thought that we were surely doomed'
It must at least be Armageddon,
Such brightness in a sky so leaden.

The storm went of for several hours
Showing nature's awesome powers
And even though it scared us some
We were impressed. It struck us dumb.

HALLOWE'EN

AJ Alexander held a Hallowe'en poetry contest for several years. This, and the ones that follow are my entries. This one won one year.

The moon has hidden her face tonight
Turned away from the Earth.
The clouds are scurrying away in fright
From what the night may give birth,
For tonight the veil is thin.

The wind is blowing the leaves around.
They hide in crannies and nooks.
Cowering, shivering, hope not to be found
By phantoms, ghosts and spooks,
For tonight the veil may tear.

Build a bonfire, create some light.
The spirits are afraid.
They like the shadows, shun what's bright
And lurk within the shade
For tonight they cross the veil.

Ghouls and spectres, wraiths and shades
Return to Earth tonight.
We're filled with dread as daylight fades.
The smallest sound will give us fright
For tonight the veil has gone.

IN THE HAUNTED HOUSE

Here's another of my entries into AJ Alexander's Hallowe'en poetry contest.

The wind it blows cold.
Like ice down my back.
I try to be bold,
But courage I lack.
In the haunted house.

It seemed such a lark
When we set off tonight.
But now it's gone dark
And we shiver with fright
In the haunted house.

Jane said. 'We'll have fun
On Hallowe'en night.'
But when slow footsteps come
She screams out in fright
In the haunted house.

'Let's take candles,' said Pete.
'More authentic for light.
And something to eat
If we're staying all night
In the haunted house.'

Jack thinks it's a game
Till the candles blow out.
Not one single flame.
He gave a loud shout
In the haunted house.

The temperature sinks.
'That means ghosts are here,'
Said Pete, who still thinks
There's nothing to fear
In the haunted house.

The door starts to creak.
It opens so slow.
Our knees have gone weak.
I wish we could go
From the haunted house.

But nothing is there
As we huddle in fear.
Not one of us dare
To get up and peer
In the haunted house.

All night there are groans.
We hear footsteps, we swear,
And the rattle of bones.
Something is there
In the haunted house.

We laugh at our fear
As we make our way home.
In daylight it's clear
No spirits do roam
In the haunted house.

The noises we heard?
Just the sounds of a house
Cooling down, and a bird
Not one single ghost
In the haunted house.

SAMHAIN

Don't go near the graveyard, darling.
Samhain is tonight.
Don't go near the graveyard, darling.
The dead will walk this night.

Keep your candle burning, darling.
Keep it glowing bright.
Keep your candle burning darling.
Be sure it gives you light.

The bonfires have been lit, darling.
To fill the dark with light.
The bonfires have been lit, darling.
Their flames reach such a height.

Put your home fire out, darling.
Be sure to do it right.
Put your home fire out, darling.
From bonfires we'll re-light.

Put food by the door, darling.
Leave it in plain sight.
Put food by the door, darling,
For our dead to have a bite.

Do not be afraid, darling.
They see that we're alright.
Do not be afraid, darling.
No harm from them tonight.

But evil spirits come, darling.
We must put them to flight.
But evil spirits come, darling.
Them we must try to fight.

Go and watch the bonfires, darling.
Stand in their bright light.
Go and watch the bonfires, darling
To keep us safe this night.

A FATHER'S HALLOWE'EN MESSAGE

And another one. Since my father died when I was very little, I wrote this from his point of view.

I Died.
I didn't want to go.
I left my wife and daughter so
I cried.

I thought
I could no longer see
All their future without me.
I fought.

I found
That each All Hallows Eve,
I could return—I need not grieve.
Not bound.

I come
To them each Hallowe'en.
They do not know. I am not seen.
I'm dumb.

They live
And I surround them both
With all my love. I am not loath
To give.

Here ends my tale.
I will be filled with endless glee
When they come to dwell with me
Beyond the veil.

MISCELLANEOUS
POEMS

A PLEA FOR PEACE

In the 1960s, people were afraid that a nuclear war was a very real possibility. After all, it had only been 15 years, in 1960, since the USA dropped a hydrogen bomb on Hiroshima and Nagasaki. It was also the era of the 'cold war', and everyone was afraid of Russia, or rather the USSR as it was then, a vast empire ruled by Russia. It was in this climate I wrote the following poem. It is the only poem that exists from that time. It is also the only poem of mine ever to have been published before as a poem and not as part of a novel. It was published in the student magazine of UMIST, in Manchester.

Now we have created something
That threatens to destroy.
One error, one mistake
And what is left for us
But Death.

I see the ruins of a country
That once was powerful.
Now it is nothing but
Ruins, dust, decay
And Death.

I hear the cries of suffering people
Many people, old and young
They cry in agony to God
Please give us peace
Through Death.

But
The only true peace we can have on Earth
Is through remembrance of our Saviour's birth.

THE NATIONAL LOTTERY

*I wrote this poem in 1992, just after the start of the national Lottery.
I had written many more during and since my student days, but this
and the previous one are the only ones to survive, unfortunately.*

No, I've not won the lottery.
Six million pounds? It wasn't me!
Not even a measly tenner.

I often think and wonder, though
If I should win a lot of dough
Would it change my life at all?
You bet it would! I'd have a ball.

First I'd go and buy a car.
(I've always fancied a Jaguar)
A BMW would be nice.
I'll buy them both and not think twice.

And then I'll get a private jet
And join the international set.
I'll fly around the world with ease
And leave this land when it does freeze.

A bigger house than the one I've got,
Another in a land that's hot.
I'd buy one on a mountain high
With snow to ski, down which I'd fly.

Expensive dresses I could buy,
And not put up that fateful cry,
'It's far too dear for me to pay
I've not enough on me today.'

I'd leave my job without a qualm
And sit at home and feel so calm.
No arguing with stroppy pupils
I'd just relax without those scruples.

But don't forget the family.
I think I'd ask them round for tea.
They'd all be there; no one would miss,
For who would lose a chance like this?

The Aunts and Uncles, cousins too,
Relatives I never knew.
They'd all turn up to take their place
In the queue to see my face.

I'd walk around the Paris shops
No job to do--my mind may rot.
I think I may be somewhat bored.
My happiness is slightly flawed.

No, I've not won the Lottery.
I hope that now it isn't me.
Perhaps a measly tenner?

ENGLAND

I was going to enter this into a competition, but in the end I chickened out.

Will always be a home to me.
The cliffs of white that guard our shores,
The rolling Downs, the bleak, cold moors,
The skylark with his liquid song
Soaring high above the throng
Of hikers, picnickers and such,
Whose hearts he never fails to touch.

The little streams and brooks do run
Through woodlands, glistening in the sun.
The little fish are swimming here;
A kingfisher is always near.
A flash of blue above the stream,
A dive, then gone, that silver gleam
Of minnows, gone to feed his brood
In holes, all waiting for their food.

In cities where the pigeons fly
The wind-blown litter flutters by.
The cars and buses, cycles too,
Line up at lights, forming a queue.
The city's clamorous roar assaults
The ears, but never, ever halts.
The busy folk all rushing past.
They never slow, time goes so fast.

The little market towns do snooze.
The slightest little thing is news.
In pretty villages with greens
Are cottages with oaken beams.
The church bells echo o'er the fields
Calling us with merry peals
As they have done for many a year
Bringing hope and lots of cheer.

This land does not a climate boast.
Just weather blown from coast to coast.
All in one day, this land can get
All four seasons, sun and wet.
Though no extremes do us attack,
Do not go out without a mac
For rain can come at any time,
Though rarely with a gale force 9.

The English folk are stubborn, too,
As we showed in World War 2.
We do not push, but stand in line,
Waiting patiently till it's time.
We do not wail and wave our arms
We think such behaviour has bo charms,
But when we're roused, then just watch out
We'll demonstrate, wave flags and shout.

And so my country is unique;
Its people never really meek.
An upper lip that's stiff conceals
A wicked humour that reveals
Our lack of deference for power,
And those who live in ivory tower.
Abroad may have its charms, it's true,
But England's magic's ever new.

CROESO Y CYMRU

Since I wrote my poem England, I decided I should write about the other countries that make up the UK. I recently returned from a holiday in South Wales, and wrote this poem on my return.

Land of the dragon,
And King Arthur's court.
Land of Myrddin
Where Magic was wrought.

Land of the Druids,
Land of the bards.
Land of mystery
Her secret she guards.

Land of song
In chapel and pub.
Land of mountains
Soaring above.

Land of beaches
Next to the sea.
Children playing,
Laughter and glee.

Land of deep valleys
Known as Cwm.
Land of coal mines
In underground gloom.

Land of the last gold
In Britain is found,
The Romans dug it
From deep underground.

Land of Eisteddfod,
Of singing and dance.
In Llangollen's valley
The whole world does prance.

Land of the Celts.
Land of the sheep.
On her green hillsides
The lambs they do bleat.

Land of the raven.
Land of the kite.
High soaring above
In graceful flight.

Land of steel.
Land of slate,
Dug from the mountains
Our roofs to make.

Land of a language
With beauteous sound.
But try to pronounce it
Your tongue will be bound.

Land of the daffodil
Land of the leek.
Symbols of Welshness
For those who do seek.

Land of green hills,
Of valleys and dales.
Croeso y Cymru.
Welcome to Wales.

SCOTLAND

Since I have written about England and Wales, I think I should write about Scotland. I recently spent a holiday in this beautiful land.

I apologise to the Irish. I do not feel I can write about your country, as I've not visited it.

Mountains strive to reach the sky.
Rushing streams down valleys flow.
This is where the eagles fly,
In high land where none do go.

Red deer, red squirrel, otters, too,
Live in this country, wild and free.
And then the hairy highland coo
Stares across at you and me.

The salmon can be seen at dawn
His scales in flashing sunlight gleam.
He strives to go where he was born:
To the headwaters of the stream.

The mist and rain fall from above.
The wild wins brings the cold and snow.
And people flock to sports they love
As down the piste on skis they go.

Scotland's beaches are pristine.
The white sands make a glorious view.
No one here to spoil the scene.
The people here are very few.

The Orkney Isles they hold the bones
Of those who came before.
The barrows and the standing stones,
And those who brave the north wind's roar.

The Western Isles they hug the coast.
The wild Atlantic breakers fall
Upon those isles, the Scots' outpost,
And beat upon the cliffs so tall.

The lowland borders gently roll.
This is a much more gentle land.
Great abbeys, built to save the soul
Lie ruined by one king's hand.

Scotland is a beauteous land,
From mountain tall to islands wild.
Its people, resilient and strong
Across the world, Scots can be found.

FIRST BORN

After the birth of my first child, I thought she was the most wonderful thing ever. Of course, all parents think that of their offspring, but I know mine was the most precious and miraculous thing to have been created.

I saw beauty when I first saw you,
My little girl, so small, so new.
Little toes and fingers small
All wrapped up within your shawl.

At first you crawled, and then you walked.
It wasn't long before you talked.
The funny little things you said
Are all stored here, within my head.

Your big brown eyes, your curly hair.
I feel such love, you are so rare.
Never was another born
Not at evening, nor at dawn.

My little girl, you are unique.
So small, dependant and so weak.
But not for long, my little one:
The years fly by and then you're gone.

Now you have children of your own
The miracle starts once again.
The love I feel for you is passed
By you, to yours, it is so vast.

The love of Mother for her Child
Is never one that's meek and mild.
It lasts forever and a day.
It never dies, come what may.

A ROMAN LEGION I

I did a little exercise one day that had been posted on a website. It said to take the seventh book on your bookshelf, open it to the seventh page, take the seventh line down and write a seven line poem beginning with that line.

The book I found was on the Roman Empire. I admit I was tempted to cheat and not use this line, but decided to give it a go. Here is my effort.

A Roman Legion also had other skills:
Engineers, builders, tailors too.
They built the roads so straight and true.
They built a wall across the hills,
Built bridges over foaming rills.
They made their clothes and built a fort
And fought the foe without a thought.

A ROMAN LEGION 2

After writing the previous poem, I decided to try a longer one. Here it is.

A Roman legion also had other skills
As well as its ability in war.
As builders Roman soldiers were not poor
And built a wall for Hadrian 'cross the hills.

When soldiers met a river, wide and deep
A bridge they built to get across the flow.
The soldiers toiled in sun or rain or snow
And if some died, well OK life was cheap.

Vercingetorix was a Celt from Gaul
Who won a massive battle, but in vain.
They soon lost all that they had gained
And Roman soldiers camped outside the wall.

The siege engines the Roman soldiers built
Bombarded all the walls around the town.
Their engineering capabilities shown
And Vercingetorix's strength did wilt.

The soldiers built the roads so straight and true
Joining all their governed lands to Rome,
Where the Emperor did sit upon his throne.
And that is why the empire grew and grew.

The soldiers sewed their clothing built the roads,
And bridges, walls and siege engines as well.
They fought and conquered as the stories tell
And beat the Celtic peoples in their woad.

The legions helped the Empire last so long.
Fighters, engineers and builders, they
Worked hard and long, they toiled throughout the day
To make the Roman Empire wide and strong.

MANCHESTER UNITED 2013-14 SEASON

I have supported Manchester United since I first knew what football was about, through thick and thin, in the good years and the bad. I remember when they went down to the old 2nd division too.

I wrote this after the first season since Sir Alex Ferguson retired. They had a disastrous season, getting knocked out of all the cups early on, and finishing only 7th in the league, thus not having European football at all in the following season. David Moyes was sacked 4 games before the season ended and Ryan Giggs took over as caretaker manager until the beginning of the next season when Louis van Gaal took over.

We missed Robin van Persie
For quite a length of time,
'Cos in the bright red jersey
In front of goal he'd shine.

Vidic is our captain.
A great defender, he.
Attackers strive in vain
To pass him and get free.

And Rio is the other one,
A partnership so great.
As centre back he always shone.
We'll miss him and his mate.

And now we see Valencia
Charging down the wing.
All opposition, they do fear
Versatility he does bring.

Rooney runs all over.
He loves to play the ball.
All the field he'll cover.
His skills do us enthral.

Our new boy is Juan Mata.
He runs in from mid-field.
The centre backs just shatter.
He shoots and they do yield.

Hernades is our Little Pea.
Yes, he will shoot on sight.
I think everyone will agree
His goals are a delight.

Our left back comes from France.
Patrice Evra is his name.
Down the left wing he does dance.
We're all so glad he came.

Our stalwart man in mid-field,
Carrick holds the fort.
The ball he never does yield.
He never sells us short.

They cannot get past Smalling.
He stops them in their tracks.
He'll give them all a mauling
'Cos he is never lax.

Now Fergie has retired.
We're sad he had to go.
But Moysie has been fired
Because we end so low.

But come on girls and boys.
We are not down and out.
Let's make a lot of noise
And with me, join the shout

Of

Glory, Glory Man United
Glory, Glory Man United
Glory, Glory Man United
As the Reds go marching on, on, on!

Hypocracy

There seem to be so many things today where people are not truly honest about what they really think. Appearances are everything. I wrote this poem to try to bring people's attention to all the hypocracy around.

We like our village churches
But we don't go there.
We love our local pub
But we don't drink there.
We don't want them to close
Though no one ever goes.

Our roads, they are congested
With cars for everyone.
The others shouldn't have them
But we, of course, need one.
It should be other folk
Who give it up and walk.

Aircraft fly above us
Polluting all the air.
We think there should be fewer
But we still fly o'er there.
We need our holiday
No matter come what may

We don't like highest earners
But want to earn as much.
We eat our meals with wine
But we don't know too much.
We really like to think
We understand our drink.

We highly praise the classics,
But we don't read them.
We talk of works of Art
But never see them.
We think we are so highbrow
But we are really lowbrow.

MODERN LIFE

As a member of the older generation, I have views about the youngsters and modern life. I wrote this poem about it.

Modern life is going clubbing.
Modern life is going pubbing.
Modern Life is fine.

Modern life is texting friends.
Modern life is the latest trends.
Modern life is wine.

Modern life is moving fast.
Modern life is slipping past.
Modern life is busy.

Modern life is working hard.
Modern life is London's Shard.
Modern life is dizzy.

Modern life is owning cars.
Modern life is visiting bars.
Modern life's a wish.

Modern life is 'All for me.'
Modern life is 'Must be free.'
Modern life is selfish.

Modern life is placing bets.
Modern life is running debts.
Modern life is tears.

Modern life is full of anger.
Modern life is full of danger.
Modern life is fears.

THE BLACKBIRD

I love watching the birds on my lawn. We have a blackbird that comes down and seems to be watching me. One day he stood before our currant bushes, looked at the ripening currents, then at me. I looked him in the eye and said an emphatic 'NO!' He looked away, then flew onto the fence. I thought, 'Ah, He's taking notice.' Then he dropped down behind the bushes where I couldn't see him! But I forgave him. He's a lovely bird.

Blackbird, searching the lawn for worms,
Your brood for to feed.
You work so hard from dawn 'till dusk
To satisfy their need.

Your glossy feathers shine so black,
Your beak is made of gold.
The brightness of your eye so clear,
Is a wonder to behold.

But over all, what we all love,
Your song so pure and clear.
The notes that tumble from your throat
Bring joy to all who hear.

They rise above, towards the sky,
And angels when they hear
Know that they have met their match
In your notes so pure and clear.

Art thou a bird or spirit free
Whose throat such notes give out?
No living creature surely makes
Such wondrous sounds, I doubt.

So are you sent from heaven above
That we on Earth might know
Something of that wondrous place
Where we're destined to go?

So, bird, keep singing out your song
At dawn, at noon and dusk
And make us feel that all that's wrong
Will turn to all that's just.

I AM EARTH

We are doing such terrible things to our beautiful planet. If the Earth could respond, would she destroy us?

I am Earth.
I am your mother.
I gave you birth.

I gave you a nest.
A wonderful home
On which you can rest.

I gave you food.
Plenty to eat.
You waste all that's good.

I gave you the seas
And forests and hills,
But you chop down the trees.

You think you're so cool,
But you pollute the air
By the burning of fuel.

You heat up the air
And care not a jot
For the poor polar bear.

Animals die
Because of your greed.
You hear not their cry.

I teemed with life,
Both great and small,
Yet extinction is rife.

Like a cancer you spread
Throughout the whole world.
It won't end till you're dead.

But I'll make you pay
For all you have done.
You'll be sorry one day.

I'll shiver my skin.
Your buildings will fall
And bury your kin.

The land I will flood
By raising the seas
And drown all in mud.

My mountains so high
Will belch forth their flames
And you will all die.

I am Earth.
I am your mother.
I gave you birth.

BUT I WILL DESTROY YOU.

WE WILL REMEMBER THEM

In 2018 there was a lot about World War 1, not surprisingly as it was the 100th anniversary. I was inspired towrite this poem in memory of my wonderful grandfather who fought in Gallipoli. I suspect that not many people know that the British troops fought there, too. We hear a lot about the brave Australian and New Zealand men, but not much about our own troops.

I'LL NEVER TRULY UNDERSTAND

How World War I began.
The death of Archduke Ferdinand
Started the deaths of many more,
The young, the old, the rich, the poor.
All died with guns in hand.

My Grandad went with Uncle Jim
And Our Poor Willie, too.
They sent them off, singing a hymn.
Grandad went to Gallipoli,
Uncle Jim left his love, Polly.
Gas in trenches did kill him.

I cannot see, in my mind's eye
Grandad with gun in hand.
A peaceful man, sent out to die.
He fought for us, for you and me
So we can live and so that we
Safely in our beds may lie.

Granddad came home, and Willie too,
But millions more did not.
Their duty they all had to do.
They died in fear, in noise, in blood.
Everything was caked in mud.
Yet in those fields the poppies grew.

The War to end all wars, they said,
So terrible were the deaths.
The youth of Europe all lay dead.
Yet 21 short years to come
Another war. Once more a gun
In young men's hands brought death.

One hundred years have passed since then.
What have we learned? Not much!
Too many men are killing men.
Wars still abound around the world.
Bombs and missiles still are hurled
At those who disagree with them.

MUSIC MAGIC

I'm a great lover of music, and learned to play the piano and violin as a child. (My mother called the latter my Vile Din, but I don't think it was that bad—or perhaps it was.) Recently my son gave me his old keyboarad and I've been re-learning to play. It's not like riding a bike. You do forget! Anyway, here's my tribute to music.

Magic winding all around
Harmonies blend
Single notes sing
And we are enraptured.

Emotions unfurl.
Magic escaping to the air.
We find that we cry.
We find that we laugh
And we are enchanted.

Stillness ensues.
We sit in silent wonder.
Magic all round.
Sound so mellifluous,
And we are bewitched.

THANKS TO ALL THE PEOPLE

During the pandemic of Covid 19, while most people were sensible and obeyed the laws set out by the Government, there were some who did not. These people inevitably contributed to the spread of the virus. I wrote this poem for them. All the events mentioned actually happened.

Since writing this, it seems that even the Government have not obeyed their own laws.

Thanks to all the people
Who broke the lockdown rules.
Thanks for spreading the virus.

Thanks to all the people
Who went to parties at New Year.
Thanks for spreading the virus.

Thanks to everybody
Who ran away from London as Tier 4 arrived.
Thanks for spreading the virus.

Thanks to everybody
Who wears masks below the nose.
Thanks for spreading the virus.

Thanks to everyone
Who fails to wash their hands.
Thanks for spreading the virus.

Thanks to the man
Who removed his mask to cough.
Thanks for spreading the virus,

Thanks to the people
Who fled Switzerland to avoid quarantine.
Thanks for spreading the virus.

Thanks to everybody
Who does not obey 2 metres.
Thanks for spreading the virus.

Thanks to everyone
Who filled the beaches in summer.
Thanks for spreading the virus.

Thanks to the people
who went on demonstrations.
Thanks for spreading the virus.

Thanks to all those people
Who kept us all indoors.

Thanks to all the people
Who ruined kids education.

Thanks to all the people
Who made life more lonely
For all those living alone.

Thanks to all the people
Who made those with mental illness worse.

Thanks to all the people
Who spoiled Christmas and New Year.

Thanks to all the people
Who flew away for a birthday.

But

Thanks to all key workers
For putting your lives in danger.
Thanks to porters, and ambulance drivers.
Thanks to nurses and doctors.
Thanks to cleaners and radiographers.
Thanks to physiotherapists.
Thanks to all who work in our hospitals.
Thanks to farmers and supermarket workers. For putting food
on our tables.
Thanks to teachers
For working hard
To continue educating children
On line.
Thanks to refuse collectors
For keeping us safe from disease.
Thanks to the police
Who continue to protect us.
Thanks to everyone who is still working.

POETRY FROM MY BOOKS

The following poems are taken from my books, primarily from The Wolves of Vimar series, Book 1, The Wolf Pack

These books are fantasy, and deal with the friendship that grows between a group of very different individuals on a quest to find a lost artefact.

All of them have come to where they are through some act of defiance and are each very individualistic people, but they overcome their difficulties to form a close-knit group, just like a wolf pack.

There are four that do not come from these books. Three are also fantasy and one from my current historical novel, Jealousy of a Viking.

DWARF WORK SONG

A fantasy poem. I decided to write it when I was writing my Wolves of Vimar Series, but it didn't get into the books.

Deep, deep below the ground
Wielding spade and pick.
Dwarven miners found
Minerals lying thick.

Tin, iron copper too,
We dig them all day long.
The solid rocks we hew
With sturdy arms and strong.

Precious stones we find.
Opals, rubies, jet.
We leave non behind.
Every one we get.

But don't you delve too deep.
Or wake the unknown there.
All kind of dangers sleep
And fearsome things lie there.

LEGEND OF GRILLON AND PARADOR

Grillon is the god of nature and wild things, and Parador the goddess of farming and agriculture. Barnat, who is also mentioned, is the god of war. The following poem is always recited by a bard at the celebrations that take place on the first day of the year, which on Vimar is the Spring Equinox. This is known as Grillon's Day. There is a religious service that takes place at the local stone circle, where sacrifices are made to Grillon and Parador to ensure good hunting and crops during the year. That is followed by a feast and dancing round bonfires symbolising Vimar's passage round the sun.

Those of you who know your Greek myths might recognise a similarity here!

One day the Lord of Nature was walking all alone
When beside a hidden pool a lovely sight was shown.
Bathing in the moonlight, where no one should have been
Was a beauteous maiden, the loveliest he'd e'er seen.

Lord Grillon lost his heart to her
This maiden oh so fair.
He vowed that she would be his own
His life with her would share.

He showed himself at once to her
As forward he did tread.
She said "And who are you, good sir?
Should you not be abed?"

Oh lovely maid, my love, my life,
I ne'er will rest again.
Unless you come to be my wife
My heart will feel such pain."

And so fair Parador was wed
To Grillon. She agreed
To always sleep within his bed
And others ne'er to heed.

But evil now will turn to dust
That love and bliss
For Barnat after her did lust
And swore she'd be his.

He poisoned Grillon's mind and said
She was untrue
That she had been into his bed
And others too.

Lord Grillon he was really sad
That she should treat him so.
He thought that he'd go truly mad
So far from her he'd go.

Now Parador had done no wrong
To deserve this fate.
She could not any more be strong
Beneath Lord Grillon's hate.

So mourn she did and all the world
Did join with her in sorrow.
All green things died and creatures curled
All safely in their burrow.

But in good time, Lord Grillon found
How false the god of war.
He came to her and he reclaimed
The love of his wife once more.

So once again the land grew green
And springtime came again.
And summer's warmth and life serene
While she forgot her pain.

And so each year the land remembers
The love of Parador,
And autumn comes and winter's embers
Till Spring returns once more.

FERO'S WORK SONG

On their way to search for the artefact, Fero, one of the companions, began to sing a song from his homeland far to the south. This is a translation of that song.

I rise before the sun each morn
And sometimes wish I'd not been born.
For life is hard here in the heat,
But I must toil or I won't eat.
And soon I will be dead and gone
But still the work goes on and on.

I plant the grain and sow the seeds.
The sun looks down on all our deeds.
His sister rain falls from above
And nourishes the seeds with love.
The sun himself gives warmth to all
And makes the plants and grain grow tall.

Now I am glad to have been born
The land is kind, it gave us corn
And grass for all our cows and sheep
And you and I can soundly sleep.
For once again through winter's chill
We'll once more live. It will not kill.

Clue found by Asphodel and Fero to the whereabouts of Sauvern's Sword. It had been written many years before and the part where it told how many people needed to go was unclear and so Asphodel wrote down the two possible numbers.

Deep in the forest lies the tomb
Protected from all evil.
Sauvern lies as in the womb,
Safe from man or devil.

His Sword is resting by his side
Awaiting call to action.
When danger lurks on every side
You need the Sword's reaction.

But first, 6? 8? questers bold must go
To Sauvern's tomb, surrounded
By Guardians strong, no fear must show
Or from there they will be hounded."

Puzzle for Carthinal to solve during his Practical test.

I actually cut Carthinal's test from the second edition of the book as I felt it did not add anything to the story and so you won't find anything about it in the current book.

Carthinal had to turn a wheel to point to the different directions in order to open a door that led to the exit of a maze. Wrongly doing so would have released a dangerous beast to be fought.

The first stanza refers to the Plains to the west, over the Western Mountains where the nomadic tribes known as the Horselords dwelt.

The second to the northern mountains known as The Roof of the World.

The third is the Great Desert in the south.

The fourth the Mountains of Doom in the East.

The spring wind blows cross mountains wide
Through land of horse where barbarians ride.

From icy mountains encased in snow
In winter do the cold winds blow.

The summer winds are soft and warm
They blow from desert and waving palm.

The autumn winds are rough and wild
They bring doom for man and child.

So turn me round and I will show
The proper way that you must go

But get it wrong and sorry be
For you must fight or you must flee.

Prophecy found by Carthinal in an old book that his teacher brought home.

When Kalhera descends from the mountains,
And orcs once more roam the land,
When impossible beasts occur
And the Never-Dying Man is once more at hand.
Then the Sword that was lost must once more be found;
Only it can destroy the threat
And kill the immortal mortal
To balance out his debt.

ELVEN EVENING HYMN

After finding the artefact, the group travelled back to their homeland via the elven land of Rindissillaran. There they heard the beautiful hymn the elves sing at dusk. Here this is in both Elvish and a translation.

Ah equillin ssishinisi
Qua vinillaquishio quibbrous
Ahoni na shar handollesno
As nas brollenores.

Ah equilin bellamana
Qua ssishinisi llanarones
As wma ronalliores
Shi nos Grillon prones.

Ah equilin dama Grillon
Pro llamella shilonores
As nos rellemorres
Drapo weyishores.

Yam shi Grillon yssilores
Grazlin everr nos pronores
Wama vinsho prolle-emo
Lli sha rallemorres.

TRANSLATION

Oh star of the evening
Shining brightly
You give us hope
In the deepening night.

Oh beauteous star
Who heralds the evening
You tell us all
That Grillon guards us

Oh Grillon's star
As you sink westwards
Return again
To guard the dawn.

Ensure that Grillon
Through darkness keep us
Safe from all evil
Until the morn.

DRAGONS FLY

I love dragons and stories containing them. Many of my fantasy books have dragons in them. This is a little poem about their beauty and danger.

Soaring high
Tiny specks up in the sky.

Dragons swoop
And loop the loop
Then come together in a group.

Dragons dive
Up there they thrive.
They all love to be alive.

Dragons flame.
It's just a game
They are wild, they are not tame.

Dragons play
Above the bay.
Dangerous beauty. Do not stay!

CRISILISK, THE RED DRAGON

More dragons. This is about a dragon that appears in my Elemental Worlds books.

> Her scales are the red
> Of sunset in autumn.
> Her eyes are the gold
> Of midsummer sun.
> Her horns of white
> Glow like snowfall in winter
> And she dances in flight,
> Like birds do in spring.

Her beauty is evident
To all who perceive her.
Her grace in the sky
Is a joy to behold.
With pinions spread wide
She dives, then she soars.
But beware; if she sees you
Her flames she'll release.

She thinks she's the queen
Of all she surveys.
All other things living
To her must bow down.
To those who refuse
To obey her commands.
She'll let loose her flames.
An inevitable end.

This poem is one recited by a skald (a kind of Viking bard) in Jealousy of a Viking, the second book in the series A Family Through the Ages. It tells of how Erik won the love of Helgha in typical Viking fashion.

Erik loved the beauteous maiden, Helgha,
The most beautiful maid
Amongst all the Danes.
Her flaxen hair flowed like moonlight on the seas
And her blue eyes glowed like the sky in summer.
But they could not marry.
Erik was promised to another.
He visited his love often
Until her father challenged him
To a battle.
Sword rang on shield.
Axe split the air with sound like thunder.
Young and strong, was Erik,
Older and wily was Biorn.
Who would win?
Youth and strength or
Guile and experience?
Biorn struck with his axe,
But Erik raised his shield.
Biorn's axe glanced off.
Erik fought bravely
Until Biorn's shield broke.
Biorn hit Erik with the edge and drew first blood.
Brave Erik did not flinch.
Blood streamed from the gash in his cheek
But he fought on, ignoring pain and blood.
The battle continued for hours
Erik parried the axe with his shield.

His sword thirsted for blood.
His eyes burned with the pleasure of the fight.
Then Erik saw Biorn tiring
The man's steps became slow,
His axe dragged
As if reluctant to hit this brave young warrior.
Erik backed into a barn wall and feigned a slip.
When Biorn came with raised axe
To finish the battle and send Erik to Valhalla,
The young warrior rolled beneath the axe
And as Biorn raised his weapon,
Erik sent his sword upwards.
Into the heart of his foe it went.
Blood flowed over both.
As Biorn crashed down, Erik rolled away.
Helgha screamed.
Her lover and her father both drenched in blood.
Who lived and who died?
Then Erik rose and seized the maiden.
He fled to Stjarna, his horse,
And leapt to her back with Helgha.
They galloped all night
Until at dawn they arrived in Jorvik.
Now Erik has a beautiful bed-slave.
And a scar on his cheek
To remind all of his bravery.

HAIKU

RAIN

I decided, to try my hand at writing Haiku. We'd just had a very rainy, wet winter and so I began with 3 about rain.

Then I thought it would be a good idea to write others about different weather phenomena. Here are the results. I hope you enjoy them.

Gentle rain, sweet rain.
Pitter-patter in the leaves
Helps the flowers grow.

The rain hammers down
Drenching the sodden ground.
Rivers overflow.

Rainbow in the sky.
The sunshine split by raindrops.
Glorious colour.

WIND

March wind howls like wolves
Stalking herds of antelope'
But I am safe inside.

Gentle breezes sigh,
Making all the flowers dance,
And wheat fields ripple.

The wind can destroy,
Downing trees and causing
Immense destruction.

SUN

The warmth of the sun,
The gentle buzzing of bees,
Tells us it's summer.

Scorching the desert.
Nothing can live in this heat
From the burning sun.

The sun smiles in the sky.
People smile on Earth below
To see him shining.

SNOW

Flakes drop gently down,
Turning all the land to white.
A magical sight.

Nothing can be seen.
Earth and sky blend into one
In the blizzard's rage.

Waking in the dawn,
Mysterious light shines in.
It snowed in the night.

FROST

Hoar frost coats the trees,
Glittering like diamonds
Dropped from the sky.

Ferns, flowers and trees
Jack frost paints on the windos.
Short-lived beauty fades.

Ponds are now solid.
Waterfowl walk on water.
The frost has arrived.

FOG AND MIST

They called it Pea Soup
Thick and yellow, blinding all
Traffic has stopped,

The mist curls all around
Swirling like smoke in the air.
All colour has flown.

Autumn brings the mist.
Dampness fills the morning air.
Dewdrops on cobwebs.

LIMERICKS

The origin of the Limerick is uncertain. I read that it was around in the thirteenth century, but the rhyming sequence was different, and so I ask, "Can they be called Limericks?"

Some sources say it came from an Irish soldiers' song called "Will You Come up to Limerick." People made up verses as it was sung.

It was made popular in England by Edward Lear who wrote his "Book of Nonsense" in 1846, although he did not call his poems limericks, but Nonsense Verse.

Wherever the name and the poems came from, they are an important part of our culture, and the form appears from nursery rhymes to songs.

Here are some of my limericks.

In a Rolls Royce driven by a chauffeur,
An enormously impressive motor,
I sat next to the Queen
Who was dressed all in green
And sporting and elegant boater.

I knew a young lady called June
Who went out to look at the moon.
She said, "This is silly.
It's really quite chilly.
I think I'll return to my room.

A poet was lying in bed
Writing limericks in her head.
She thought that she should
Write down what was good
Before her ideas went dead.

A woman who came from West Ham
Once rowed in a boat on the Cam.
When she passed by the Backs
And heard the ducks' quacks
She rowed into the bank, bam, wham, slam.

One day as I played my violin
The door opened and Mother came in.
She said with a frown,
"Please put that thing down.
Nobody likes your vile din."

Difficult maths is my pride.
I can solve it when others have cried.
Cone volume divining,
Circle area refining.
I think you can say it's pi-eyed.

If you enjoyed these poems, please leave an honest review.

Perhaps you would like to visit my blog at http://aspholessari-a.wordpress.com/
I occasionally post some poetry there as well as other bits of my writing, book reviews and help with spelling and grammar.

If you enjoyed the poetry from The Wolf Pack and would like to read the book, you can buy it from https://books2read.-com/u/m0lxE: It is available from a number of platforms, and this link will send you to your favourite seller.

It is also available as an audiobook.

To the English teachers who struggled with me throughout my school days.
They were wonderful people who taught me how to write well, both prose and poetry, and about the rules of grammar that have stood me in good stead in my writing career.
I suspect none of them would have imagined I would end up writing novels and poetry!

ABOUT THE AUTHOR

 V.M. Sang lived in the north west of England in a little town called Northwich where she went to school until leaving to train as a teacher in Manchester. Here she studied Science, Maths and English.

V.M. enjoys music, and has recently taken up playing the piano once again. She is a great fan of JS Bach and has visited Germany, following in his footsteps.

Visiting historical places, like Rome, Split, and places within the UK is a great pleasure to V.M. These visits have given her background for her historical novels.

When not writing or travelling, V.M. watches sport, and is a life-long supporter of Manchester United. She also does a variety of crafts, painting and drawing, and enjoys walking and nature.

She is married with two children and three lovely grandchildren.

To learn more about V.M. Sang and discover more Next Chapter authors, visit our website at www.nextchapter.pub.

Miscellaneous Thoughts
ISBN: 978-4-82415-784-3

Published by
Next Chapter
2-5-6 SANNO
SANNO BRIDGE
143-0023 Ota-Ku, Tokyo
+818035793528

25th November 2022

Lightning Source UK Ltd.
Milton Keynes UK
UKHW011834161222
414070UK00003B/121